PELICAN

Emily O'Neill

YESYES BOOKS PORTLAND

COVER ART AND DESIGN BY DANIEL OBZEJTA

INTERIOR DESIGN BY ALBAN FISCHER

AUTHOR PHOTO BY JONATHAN WEISKOPF

FIRST EDITION, 2015

ISBN 978-1-936919-30-7

PRINTED IN THE UNITED STATES OF AMERICA

PUBLISHED BY YESYES BOOKS

4904 NE 29TH AVE

PORTLAND, OR 97211

YESYESBOOKS.COM

KMA SULLIVAN, PUBLISHER

HEATHER BROWN, PUBLICIST

JILL KOLONGOWSKI, MANAGING EDITOR

STEVIE EDWARDS, ACQUISITIONS EDITOR

JOANN BALINGIT, ASSISTANT EDITOR

AMBER RAMBHAROSE, ASSISTANT EDITOR

ROB MACDONALD, CO-EDITOR, *FREQUENCIES*

MARK DERKS, FICTION EDITOR, *VINYL POETRY*

PHILLIP B. WILLIAMS, POETRY EDITOR, *VINYL POETRY*

ALBAN FISCHER, GRAPHIC DESIGNER

JOHN MORTARA, SOCIAL MEDIA EDITOR AND WEB DESIGN

FOR SEAN & PEDRO

Kismet

But.

There is an onion
browning where my heart should be.

A boy who bakes pies,
a bottle of liquor finished in a single sit.
Nothing so warm
stays that way.

But—gracious
hesitation//reverse thrust—costume change
from bow-legged fawn to winged singer.

Walk home from the city line
with a knife pressed to my bare thigh:

I dare
the dark to eat me fiercely,

butterzone drunk, grinning,
my glowing teeth
graveyard candles.

But: a gifted grace.

I sing sorrow turned to syrup, skinny
dip in the chilly Atlantic, drink tallboys,
dance with the bouncer. Flounder.

But broken skin knits together
without itch & scab flakes off
my sudden feathers.

... for never did mother-sheep love her lamb as the pelican loves its young. When the young are born, the parent bird devotes all his care and thought to nourishing them. But the young birds are ungrateful, and when they have grown strong and self-reliant they peck at their father's face, and he, enraged at their wickedness, kills them all. On the third day the father comes to them, deeply moved with pity and sorrow. With his beak he pierces his own side, until the blood flows forth. With the blood he brings back life into the body of his young.

GUILLAUME LE CLERC, 13TH CENTURY CE

When God Dies He Hands Me the Keys to the Castle

If I could, I'd tell the story with silence—a stage of bones
      sunk into trench, driftwood puppet, orchestra of radios

gone quiet with the waiting—but
      silence is a half-blooded thing

& no one knows how to keep it. You cannot
      pour it into a jar & hide it in a storm cellar.

You cannot ask silence to grow hooves,
      to gallop across sand with you on its back.

It cannot carry you. It will not sit like a blaze on your forehead,
      marking you chosen. Will not slow you with stillness

like a dragged lake or drowned fish. Often, I am not the woman
      I want to be. If grief is a house, it's made of stone.

When I ask God *What will it feel like to be dead?*
      He says *Nothing. You will not feel it.*

God's body stops like a watch
      unwound. A Halloween ghost draped in a sheet.

His hands folded like an unsent letter.
    Jaw wired shut, blood drained, organs gone

gray with wait. Time is light enough to wound me
    mortally. Loss is living alone with east-facing windows.

I wake in the morning with no one there to record it. A tree fallen in
    the forest
    is not dead. It is still green, blanketed with tiny green shoots.

Sea Gate

When I was a seven, I saw a man die.
The ocean fell out of his mouth.
I told my father, but he didn't believe me.

Daddy, I saw him.
If we die, does that mean
we go sailing?

My father has died clinically seven times.
He swims up through sedatives,
asks us where he is,

what has happened. Bags of saline dangle
over the bed. A storm tears into trees
beyond the window. My father, fallen

asleep with his mouth open. I cannot look:
his parted teeth, a gate unlocked.
I am still convinced that when we die

it is liquid. The ocean falling
out of a man's mouth.
When my father dies

people will ask. I will
point to the sea.

Caught in Bruce's Mouth

We spent my first *Jaws* summer landlocked
which was good, because the fear wore off
quick. I replaced it with close study.

How the size? Why the jaw? Jersey
beach terror of 1916. Bull. Rogue. Frenzy.
My father said the sound went mostly empty

the year the fiction broke. Shaw wrote
his own monologue. Indianapolis capsized,
ocean a sharp grave: death by thirst,

death by salt, death by shark. No beach
for me. Just a lake's mucky lips. Lucas's head
caught in Bruce's mouth. Amity's hysteria,

a spring wound back on itself. I sat, rapt,
hungry for the jerk and pull and scream.
Tape trapped in the VCR—rewinding.

Buying Flowers in the Lobby Gift Shop

Yellow cab carousel. Wheelchairs
abandoned curbside. Sloppy portraits
of street signs, cloud animals. Linoleum
crowned with kinetic sculpture—
billiard balls spun down a knotted track,
an unending Rube Goldberg machine.

Visitor's pass, elevator hallway,
a dozen floors vanish too fast
for my body. Confused traffic
like ants under the bridge
between wards. A dead pigeon
on the carpeted floor, hiding
its face under a wing.

The nurses smile, wait
with Oreos, rubber gloves inflated
into stegosaurus balloons. They won't speak
above a whisper, *need more tests*,
reach across me to inject. A guessing
game. I answered right. My father,
so happy, they've drugged him sleeping to stop his
teeth, their cracked smile. My mother
picks wilted blooms out of the vase,
drops them in the trash.

How I Am Not My Mother

To be only bone. To be thin
chrome handle bars on a quiet bicycle.
Small & held like a pebble
underneath my tongue, assassin
of thirst. She used to run, before
all of the children. She used to be
knife fine. I saw a picture
of her glowing frown, her hips
with their ashtray curves. Muse
at dock's end, endless black olive hair.
That's what they called her:
Olive Oil. Angular, and animated.
I tore my voice off trying
to be uncanny, porcelain.
I want to be the same ghost.
I jog around the block,
a gasping hole in my sail.
Force my feet into tiny
wooden shoes and bleed.
Hope to become a lens
flare. A stoic.
Like her.

Inheritance

Dining room birds of paradise. Cocktail shrimp.
I tried on Mom's gown at fifteen; already

too small to zip past my hips. Paint it
red. Brick or birth or a pick-up that you used to drive.
We kept the keys. Paint it that living

color I see at *swelling, asphyxia, inheritance.* The check
arrived the day before yesterday. One-thousand-eight-hundred-

and-nine dollars, shotgun for the wedding. No father-
daughter dance. Confession: I had a baby once, I can't forgive
myself or the drink that bled him from me.

What does a riverbed look like from the other side?
Could I walk to you? Will the tide turn our color?

I am my father's daughter. I won't cry,
can't unclasp my bones like fingers
folded to a fist post-prayer.

Suckerfish

They say it is important to keep busy.
To have hobbies. I do these things
but nothing shifts. I can pretend I am an animal

but it's mostly a lie. I do have busy, feral hands.
I am sorry. Finding my way towards rot is a constant
accident, and stories come out of my mouth
before I have time to dress them
in more acceptable clothes. I left my tomboy body

on the blacktop
with a sore to pick and now she bleeds
into the present tense. Each bruise, another jaw
around me in the dark.

Virage

If it's still a restaurant
let's never go back there.
Let's speak only in the code
used by teens who collect Schnabel quotes

& forego sex because who has the time?
There are so many worthless people
waiting to be insulted. Tell me all about them.
Pretend we're at the Seville before the smoking ban.

That's how the coffee we've made tastes, so bitter
that it gives me hiccups. I'm laughing because we learned
to kiss how I learned to drink my coffee black.
What if I had stayed in Catholic school or drawn our hands

hundreds of times, layered triangles of broken
knuckle? Shadow birds. Rabbit tangrams.
Another week of cake for lunch daily with a boy I loved
who loved me. But I have no sweet tooth

& it's better to burn than be touched. Pretend
when I say my parents are a Springsteen song
it isn't because I ran away to Manhattan every weekend
trying not to unlock the same luckless room.

Before the Elegy

I wanted him gone
hard and bright. The kind death
afforded by a car crash or bullet,

not that coward needle. This slow swell
feels nothing like dignity. When the heart is weak,
it goes to war with itself. I fuck, hoping

pleasure will push grief from my body,
let me sleep. But dreams
set me walking: my father,

a silent film, now mute of his stories.
The last man who gave me
flowers will never meet the first.

I run a length of tiled hallway,
find machines choking
them both, my love

strangled by effort to save it.
My eyes fall out of my head.
I turn over. We collect crabs

from the tide line. My father says, *Don't stay.*
I turn over, collapse at my own wedding.
Find six wax-white mummies beneath pear trees,

one for each death's visitation.
I cut off a finger, bury it at sea.
I wake up alone. Draw a bath of war paint.

I want an accident, an instant.

Wishes for the Full Moon

North Amherst new
with waist-high corn.
Our beds unmade,
unframed. Bike chains hung
over the porch railing &
Molly's cherry red convertible.
The neighbors tell stories about heroin
& both of us are afraid & eating
nachos, Muhammad
Ali, a swarm of wasps
on the apartment wall.

Pass that summer through a filter of blue
light: flame & wink & lightning.
Pond water pealing across naked skin.
We were eternal. I dyed
my hair blonde; the bleach didn't burn this time
but the bathroom felt like fire at the shoulder

of a borrowed field. Here we are in the city
now. No yard trapped in cracked amber.
No heaven when the wind combs us
clean. If only I could show you
where I was alive.

The Ballad of Sexual Adventure

That first time, I lay
on a trampoline
with his hand
down my cut-offs,
excused the action
with a sigh of summer
& another long-drawn
breath to follow. *Don't go
to sleep, why you gotta
go to sleep* when the dark
unfolds like petals
under heat summer
summer—exhale—expand
to fill the gaps between
stars fallen silent, dark,
another hole
in the sky's sparse light.
The answer to every opening
must be *yes* & so I said it
without thinking
& fell open like a flower
one day closer to the dead.

Roadkill

Repeat my father's unfamiliar language: *quick*
pick on the Pick 6. My first lottery. All hope

hung on a receipt. Two clips of voice
saved—I replay the mumbled joke and tax advice

in my Cutlass, windows rolled up,
an aquarium of sound.

Cross a bridge—the water's him.
Sing: my throat is his—a rippling flag.

I am too calm. How can I be afraid
with death close as cold in my bones?

Healed, the pot I watch,
knowing it will never boil.

Cicada

Those two weeks live still in my throat
tar-slick, burnt. I'd dreamt it—the end of summer—a match
dead from rain. The boy built a statuary of my sins while I slept.
All the virgin parts of me that no longer bleed.

How sudden the body. How far from the mind
we stray, stolen from hope. We pushed through
the reservoir fence, fucked for the fourth time
that night. The world twitched like an insect.
The shell crumbled off from heat—red strands of hair
in denim pockets, three burn scars on my forearm
where I blistered. A hiccup
growing legs, kicking my ribs from the inside

until I came, biting the back of his hand. To whom
do the near-sighted pray? To skin. Undressed
by teeth and now, nothing left for the fingers.

Knife Play

the fastest way
to cut a man

         say
      you weren't here
         first

use your open
palm

         conjure
    back the branding iron—
      cocoa, shining
windowsill   High Lives
I ground against

        who taught
       you that

woman he stole
false history
suspended

        between
     flight & skinned
       knees
slap him til he cuts
new teeth

        parlor trick
     right card drawn

red in the cheek
red, fresh meat   of diamonds
                        of hearts

          say   I've won
     you weren't   already
     the only one   pretty, pretty

                    don't worry
        your pretty little head

Under Fresh Growth

The full moon
        is a cheesecake gone warm,
last of the homemade whipped cream
        runny over breakfast
   strawberries. No one eats.
              The cream separated
      in the fridge.
The kitchen reeks of spoil.
                  Old home movies
        slide through the projector
    at the wrong pace. Everyone looks happier:

     my mother, beaming,
         hand on her swollen belly,
             my brother
       in his underwear,
    my grandmother's heels,
      my face the same
    as my sister's,
  and my sister's
      skinned knees, freckles,
   my father's un-flecked hair,
his unburdened smile.
               The past few years have been
           straight summer,

never snow on Christmas,
a still, uncomfortable
85 degrees
long past midnight.

The lawn mower has been broken
for weeks.
There is clover mixed
with the crabgrass now,
jump cut, heat lightning,
mosquito welts.

I twist stalks of rhubarb
out of the garden
& behead them.

Bridge & Tunnel

The upright laughs at my idiot hands.
    Peter, a paper crane.

Mel dragged us to his studio from the bus stop, took our picture.
    We, pair of flightless birds tacked to my wall.

Writing to say I walked away barefoot. Eyes are not
    the only sense. Shredded sneakers, Fort Lee.

              The car got towed.
              He wouldn't
              let me photograph
              his face. Stop sign.

A box of strangers
for the lawn: (maybe one
is you)
              Honeysuckle.
              Forsythia. Newsprint,
              oil, turpentine.

    Pierogi. Pineapple upside-down cake.
Lemon-stung fingers. Slice, squeeze—screwdrivers.

Paint cakes, dirty water
hot dogs, fireworks,
backs to the FDR—

I can't divine lonely from the glimpses I get. Each minor key, razor
wire. Manual transmissions stall (I'll never
learn). Shaking a Polaroid slows the reaction
that produces the desired image.

We played a lot with light. Every portrait
a blur of his palm.

Sense Memory

He left his scarf in my purse
and I wore it all week
just for the scent of him.
Scallops. Smoke. The wine
that stained our tongues. I take this
currency to bed with me, sleep in a nest
with the ghost of our sweat, lament changing
sheets on laundry day. The road home
becomes a simple question:
the crackle of almost-snow
where I was pulled over past Worcester,
the 7-11 where we pried open the car's bent hood
to feed her another quart of oil,
the alley behind Local Burger
where I lifted my dress to show him
the tops of my stockings. My skin blooms
with lost proximity—bruises smaller
than new purple irises. The memory of eye teeth
in my shoulder. The print of his rushed thumb
on my wrist. Forgive my stumble.
All I know of falling is finding the ground.

Manic (Unbridled)

Tonight in the shred of rest
  I coax down my throat
I dream a dappled horse eating from my outstretched palm
    & the beast looks like a caught rain
      cloud you could sink into like the sea & sleep stays
        20 minutes tops before

                my body wakes
    me against reason because there's furniture to move
    & clothing to discard & 3 weeks of dinner to cook then freeze
   & the rioja wasn't gone when I left the kitchen so I find it
     & drink & the time wasn't long from light again
  so why waste another empty hour thrashing
    in my deeply empty bed

       but as I braid & unbraid
  my dirty hair, the kitchen smells like apples
    & I'm crying over an appaloosa (a name that's been wound
round my tongue since I was a fizzing child) & the rain won't come
    & it's too dark for clouds
   & that horse may as well be the moon
for how constantly it haunts me asking *when will you ride again?*
  when will storm carry you away?

Truces for the New Moon

Remember when you bled
for a month without clotting?

This venom is worse than
infection, anger inflected

in the toilet's endless run,
in the stove's cackling

refusal to light. If you dream
deeply, you can see the other side:

the cast iron perfectly seasoned,
your hair long and its silver

cast lavender in the right light.
Even if the milk in the sky is sour

it will not always be so. Cast
your lot with the living.

Don't let spite draw you a bath.
Go to bed on gritty sheets

and love him. The nights will brighten.
The house will change shape

and swallow you both. Set the seed
on the sill. Call the monster,

the dark, by
its temporary name.

On Giving Up Your Ghost

I could crawl inside another tongue, simple
sloop, absent its season of fatherly love. Brendan
and I hewed a ship she'll keep in the crook of her arm
like a lily. My lady kisses my left check. Embroiders me
golden. (necklace clasp, dead leaf) Sailing
on a lake's not sailing. There is no such gale.
I found a litany in ripples. How she says
nothing while she moves her lips, how I argue
against retreat. Each molar holds a secret:
how truth and spite flower from the same bitter root.

Stitches

Dad and I had cussed the room sizzling,
fled the kitchen like a pair of startled birds.

I escaped in Matty's van. Dad made for the bus station, tripped
over the train tracks that fenced in our street. A chunk of gravel

sheared a hole through his ear. My mother brought him
back to the house, talked him into getting stitches.

They drove to the ER while I snuck into a movie without paying,
laughing until the intake of breath stabbed and stabbed.

My sister said I was wrong to hate Dad
that way: out loud, to his face, teeth bared.

Slipped the word *cunt*
between my ribs and twisted the blade.

When I was little and he hit me, he was always still
wearing his watch. He lost his vision, his legs,

the impulse to treat us like colts—all his violence to time.
When I was old enough something wild

bubbled ugly in me and I slung it at him, every chance.
We both ran away from home. Both of us. I can't forgive the details,

how many twitching hands it took for my voice
to break. To know what it looks like to hurt a man

instead of falling over his knee. Or the black, bloody thread
holding him closed and close to me, the story I tell only to myself.

Teeth Dreams

I.

It has been the same cave
since I learned to remember
& a set of hands emerging
from a tear in the darkness.
Running, always, deeper
towards heat but no light.

II.

My love is naked with a woman who is not me.
She eats him like an apple, pares flesh from the skin
until he's only ribbons of tattoo: black eagle,
the cogs of a clock. The boy who wanted to stay
forever. The boy made only of bone.

III.

My high school
English teacher (the love
letter I didn't open) breathes into my ear,
says *Snow White waking with a kiss means coitus*;
says he hates me for growing into my anger,
for wearing it like a gown.

You need a man,
he says, taking both my hands.

IV.
This time, I am naked
in bed with a woman
& I do not know
where to begin.

V.
Apple seeds are born from cyanide
but I've swallowed a few
& never died.

Experts insist
it is impossible to die in a dream
but I've died on a mammoth's tusk,
in the river, when my car erupts in flame,
as a tulip in between doe's teeth.

Death is never impossible. What's impossible
is love passing away from me. I'm not fast enough
to close each window before the storm, to sit down
& count the seconds between lightning
flash & thunder. Count the reasons
I could never leave.

Pushed

An apple seems too perfect
a symbol. Try the fruit's path

from branch to hand to mouth:
how the skin's blush ties knots.

Try the odd snake, vibrant
muscle, one length of a wrong

tongue. What of God? Absence
speaks louder than a low-down hiss.

Draw an outline around it. Call it
the Devil. Temptation is not teeth

through sin. Try the tree. It's easy to fall
climbing. One wrong foot, a promise broken.

Proof

When you're too young to know it
your body is already deciding

what gets abandoned. Not every night
will end up memory. Quiet fades,

an at-home dye job. Once I was auburn
and swisher sweet, ankle deep in pool water

telling Amanda boys don't know how to kiss
until she said *prove it* so I did but

I can't currently remember touching her,
only the handfuls of plain Cheerios I ate all weekend

at her parents' house, how I fell asleep during *I ♥ Huckabees*,
how her boyfriend didn't think it odd when he found us both

in her bed, not naked, or even close to compromised,
but quiet in a language he would never speak.

Times of Grace

When her name begins
a sentence, the story
won't start
                without fracture.

        I unravel
the distance between. Caffeine
            tightened teeth, sugared night
                    drives. Cracked cement
            pool, library floating
            in flooded cellar.

The after dark.
            The Porterhouse. Prying the safety
                    from her lighter. *Sid
                    and Nancy*, a lullaby.

        I separate the memories
so they can't argue.

        She says
her grandmother has two
Bell Jar first editions,
            that she'll steal one for me.
                    Leads me to the kitchen,

her hands over my eyes,
to a green-keyed '61 Remington
Portable.

I have seen her
dressed as other selves
and I do not believe
them.
I choose these times of grace. Her owl
eyes unmasked. No hint of where we
break. Circling a single question

too dangerous to attempt:
Who loves you more than me?

The Right Words

My sisters play *Sorry* on the floor, take turns drawing cards that might
send them home. The nurses climb over their game to check his vitals.
I pad around in socks for two days as if wandering the dorms at college.
They warned his heart would burst my freshman year. He lived through
graduation; I refused to walk. I am a monument to a shrunken god.

There is an hour where he gasps so hard, we are sure. No green beating
mountain range on a monitor, only his breath—shallow sea with fickle
tides. Every book I've read this month kills a father.

March Fourth

When he's gone (always) the day is a snapshot
series. Postcards:

        my new home's tallest building is the Westin,
     steaming milk is like finding a radio station, I recognize
        beers by how their bottles break.

    I don't dream him
at the threshold. Open mouth, a lockless city.

Nor the chips of bones in that heavy bag of ash.
      Can you kill a ghost with fire?

              The train conductor calls BACK
BAY and I'm awake. I have no secrets. I lose every lottery.
My scalp tingles when I stare at strangers.

The sun isn't a quitter; sweat stains my seams; I'm not
a flowering tree. I would tell him all of it.

              But how?

        Is he the reason that the kettle won't sound
     when it boils? The dead seem present

in the winter—windows trace them
in the frost. But this season,

                           no snow in New England. Will he visit
anyway? (Pour three fingers of rye. Sing
        a song we know in passing.)

        This time of year, the clouds get fickle. I remember
a drought when my father took army showers, how he said

it shouldn't take more than a gallon of water to get clean.

Born to Die

Let's go get sad. Cry the road wild.
Get down pouring rain blind, Montana

black as a door-jambed finger. Let's choose
our last bad man at the next truck stop,

twist him like stem from cherry before the pie,
tear him from skin like a Band Aid.

The mountains, like us, are fallen women.
I pray they keep me shameless.

Our mothers forgot to pray us good again. We grew up
scorched, are the same black smoke, burnt as the Badlands.

Last I heard my coast say *come home* I kept driving.
The horizon is a donkey when it kicks us in the teeth.

We tumble past heart-shaped sunglasses, blue ribbon
anything. Outrun our shadows until we meet them new

on the other side of a wasted night
when the truck seizes & I pledge

allegiance to my dad with every whiskey swallow.
Gold coins of light. Trip sevens. Las Vegas, like hell,

is just south of now. How many times
can we die embalmed in stars?

Litany for the Waning Moon

There can be no discoveries. Stones
all turned, my lip snarling
away from teeth. Lift off. On my back,
engine tearing through the atmosphere.

Turmoil to keep the coals stirred and still burning.
Space: a quiet dark, a room you pass through
but don't stop to visit, empty measured
with outstretched arms. Ocean sucked away

like smoke. There is no hurt dancing
towards me, only inky darkness full of sparks.

Flint where I am guilty.
Fire where I am guilty.
Light where I am guilty.

I'm ready to be smacked out of the sky.

The Coffin Letter

I watched his tongue dry up,
no more sound
from liar's lips. Only
the lisp of hospice.

I will never know what he looks like
dead. He was ash before I thought to ask.
We fed him to the Hudson near the giant steps,
that ancient rope swing. I saw my mother choke
and wanted a different story. He died

a naked king, willed me horse's legs.
Each night, I am ridden by the hearts
of men who don't grow old. I buck,
throw them in the hopes that they will break
before I do.

Phone Call with the North End

Between my pillows, that sailor song
voice rolls in like a fog over the bay.

I can hear every moment
we've spent smitten in the breath
flanking sentence: onions sizzling in the kitchen,
jangling sock full of laundromat quarters, stiff
spring wind along the Charles that warmed
at first sign of our skin.

The first time that we met I was asleep.
This is how I know he is important.

When he dozes off, I whisper
in the trough between snores
that he is a tooth meant for a gap in me.
There are spaces in him that will sink us.

I leave hope like a coin
in the throat of a lucky well.

We Are All Wolves

Killing moon and a spade in my fist.
      I tell myself, *be an open span of turned earth*, a furrow
          untapped by roots. Better to tell the truth
     that comes when called, like blood becomes a lake
beneath the skin. All the concrete talk I've practiced, false.
     The howl will always twist past teeth.
          Eager, essential. No consonants rise
in my chest. Only stretched vowels that mean sinning.

Better to believe in a sprawling
     loneliness, like a gutted city
          or a river fat and falling over
damside. Better open up and say,
     I am no better than a long and pealing
          scream. Jagged,
how I crumpled under the August sky
     hot with night birds, trilling.

When I deny that I'm wild
     a once green part of me goes gray.
          Little bones, white crumbled shells.
     Little stones skipped across water,
only I can feel their ripples in my lungs.
     Who told me to hide from the fierce spaces that built me?

Instinct won't die by a bullet.
Won't burn, bury,
tame, or thrill, or
kill its young for food.

Salting the Earth

Grieving leaves me curiously
deformed, an ugly spectacle

for those who can't swallow swords.
Drinks are never strong enough.

People ask vulgar questions, vultures
circling my uncanny luck. I crave a missing cat,

a burning barn, some other reason
to salt the earth. There are cornfields I've pissed in

west of here. Highways that know
my body better than my bed.

Fall in a city does not
smell the same. I prefer

the furrows of shit.

Wage Slave

My paycheck is a pittance. I try not to cry
until after work. I spend the afternoon
face down in the dark, humming a song
for the failure of minimum wage. The ashtray
and the aching ankles. Rice and beans
and rice and beans. The memorial service
I will miss. My father's two black eyes.
What little hope lies in an unmade bed.
What a little hope I am. Slave of the second shift.
This week when I drive to Portland, they'll rent a stage
and I will finally sing the words: what little hope
in the lies of a half-made girl. At least
enough to chart a course by. I can roll
the sun across the sky, a dung beetle.
Despair is an ancient god. I am not
the first priest to make sacrifices.

On the Day You Decide You Are Quitting

No one has baked you a cake with *Exit Strategy* written in blue icing beneath rapidly melting candles. But quick—before they're out—make a wish. For a year of Sundays, a scuttled alarm clock, permission to sleep infinitely. Wish for a used car and a road trip, for the sequoias, for floating on the ocean like a pelican, mouth brimming with stories. Admit you have been traveling towards yourself for years. You will meet yourself in the middle of the road in the center of your country where the land is an ancient mattress and both of your selves are marbles destined to meet and meet, again, again in all of the cities that pull at your heart. No celebratory main street parade, but you are a balloon now, floating high above all of the gray people at gray desks moving invisible things from one column of a document to the next. Balloons do not have jobs. Their only marketable skill is escape.

Disguises for the Waxing Moon

I cried the first time
I saw a woman skin a rabbit,
        her efficient hands
            oiled by death.

        I've done it too—dissolved
into the trees, become an unlikely predator.

Once you call
yourself a hunter, you will never stop
shooting your own shadow, scattering like birdshot,
           like the sudden glut of feathers clogging my mouth
               when I wake pressed into the pillow.

His eyes flutter & his mouth hangs
slack as the clapper in a bell. Love song
for rock salt in the doorway
& a shotgun.

        I see him, fallen
      open. The way sleep unlocks a man.
If there is a Clyde in him—rounded
    shoulders, cocked hip,
        a hesitator—I will take him to the vault,

turn out my pockets, key open each secret
as if there is no approaching danger.

Amiss

Each room at the party is a ghost. Peel back
the fresh scab—*do you miss him,*

    tell me which part died first / will you cry if we conjure in detail

                These are things we don't discuss.
        Instead, Cassandra taught me to eat raw mushrooms,
            to hold silence in teeth, let it die there.

        In Detroit, someone insisted on grace. I found ten
    crescent moons in her palms after dinner.

All his stories, gone—
    departure, both sudden and slow.

        A person's light is blinding until
        they pass, pulling all after them.

              I'm cattails
          leaning towards the train.
          Cass and I are lost boys
              hiding.

Who would ever want to grow this way?
Who could ask to unwrap loss like a gift
only to find it plain and ragged?

I say *no* to past tense. Keep up "is," call him still-living.

There come times I hold Cass closer than kin,
carry her dirt on my back, follow her to the highway.

There must be somewhere we could run to with fireflies in winter,
voices unfurled like our old men after wine, some wild comfort
gathered close like rock pulling at the tide.

If justice exists, she'll find her father's urn broken in an earthquake.
We threw my dad in an ugly river when it was done.

The Pour

Sean & I slink
down to my Buick
with the green
handle of funeral
whiskey & 2 mason
jars. Into my coffin
with the death

drink. Rain, pouring
the car door closed
on loss. I sip & smoke
alongside stories,
chasers for the hearse
we didn't have
in July. We kill the thing.
One final dip of wrist. Talk

through ghostly haze. Absence,
threadbare shroud.
Pity, invitation
for a lonesome party.

Sip & smoke. Say
& say. Layered
shots of when, & why,

where, & who. The names
mix & they marry. I float
face down in past

flesh: it lets me
touch the living
without shame.

Nursery

I found a shark tooth in the garden.
I planted it in a bowl of dirt and waited. Two days
later, a tiny gray sprout; two weeks
and it flowered, the color of clouds threatening rain.
I made a cutting just before it opened,
set it in a vase on the kitchen table.
Everyone said they'd never seen a flower
that shade that wasn't already dead.

Clearing dishes after dinner one night,
I saw something swimming around the stem.
I stopped up the bathtub and poured out the vase.
The swimmer leapt from the water to bite
the flower as it fell. It ate every petal.
I closed the curtain around it
and went to bed.

In the morning, I awoke to a wet slap.
I ran to the bathroom and forced open the door.
On the floor, the blonde-skinned, tiny-eyed sea dog
thrashed in a puddle, gills gasping, nose pointed
towards the ocean. As if it could smell
where it had not been born.

Rusalka

My body turns
wrong. I find it inland.
A valley.   Have to drive
                        to the river.
          Have to hurry my knees
      bird, fly like a ghost
          growing scales.

      Half snake,
half maiden. Skinny simple child
          too quiet for myth. If I'm dead
                    it's because I've been carved
                        from the coast.
Skinny & sunk, wrong turn & I slip
      siren, no   island, no
                    violent   cutlass
                        casting shadow on a throat.

                    Stuff me down in standing
          water. Test the law to see if it breaks
                    when you push.
          Quarry lookout point   a woman's body
the window
      to climb out of.
      If I want to run

I give up my tongue. Gut, clean. If I want to run
    I must stop this retelling.   Stories
                grow up fast, like fish.

        He said
       Italy, told me dropping
      acid 3 times a week
    at least, said cocaine bumps hidden
      in the recessed filter of a Parliament
              cigarette. He's worried
      his molars down to silt.

I turned wrong, am stuck in his beak
    too big to swallow whole.   Skinny violent myth.
            Knife his heart & I'll get back
              my sisters.
  If I'm dead I'm shrouded in a flood of white
    satin falling over me like foam.
        My hair, gone green
      & I'll kill him   for hooking me by the mouth.

        If I'm dead I've forgotten
        slaughter.

      The water eats
      women.

        I offer me up.

No Older

I saw his girlfriend's breasts on the internet.
    They're lovely—larger than mine—
        & turned Sunday's sun
        milky. Only whiter
        span, the sheets.
        I closed my eyes
        & then the blinds
        & then the browser tab
        after a harlot pause.

We meet downtown. The entire city is an unfamiliar bar
    with a TV-ready name. Peculiar Pub, then
        Kettle of Fish where I can't catch
        the barman's eye. Taking my elbow,
        he says *You're a good person.*
        We leave the tab open.

At worst, he's become a stranger. Muscular,
    with a sudden smoking habit. But come on
        closer—he's no older
        than the day we last fought.
        History is ugly this way.

I'm a good person. I didn't breathe on his neck
    when we said goodbye or steal his hand

or blush at our bodies
stitched Siamese where
the cab lurched crossing
the Manhattan bridge.

Mated

He and I are playing chess in the belly of a whale, and he is losing. I can tell he knows this: he chews his sweatshirt zipper pull, makes moves without looking up from the board. The whale lists; its moans are amplified when heard from the inside. The white queen takes the black rook, putting the king in check for the third time.

He stares at me through foggy glasses and asks if I'm happy when I write love songs. I can't answer. I take another of his pawns. The whale's stomach smells better than I expected it to, like a sushi restaurant. We went for sushi once, when we were first friends. He taught me how to use chopsticks. *Like this*, he said, and the polished bamboo stretched from his hand like an ibis beak, trained to extract even the smallest grain of rice and present it to me like a rare pearl.

The whale lurches and he catches me from falling into its heaving side. The chess pieces roll off the table and through scattered puddles on the soft pink floor. He is still waiting for my answer. *I used to think the pickled ginger they put on the plate was lox.* He laughs, and I can't tell if it's because he thinks I'm artless, or because he's relieved about his king, now floating safely near a headless fish.

He kisses me through his fingers as a thick swell of water rushes down the whale's throat, knocking us off our knees into a soup of bishops and krill and sand.

The Age of Instability

When Winona says,

have you ever confused a dream with life?

I wander into Sean's apartment
for the first time. He hands me a High Life—
welcome to college—and we joke
about how depression has come
conveniently into fashion.
Miss the train? Kill yourself.

When Brittany carved herself
so thin she vanished,
my doctor prescribed the drug that killed her
and Sean said *at least you'll be skinny.*
Eighteen was my mistake, but twenty-four came slowly
over him, too much champagne. The pair of us,
psych ward salt and pepper shakers.

Susannah says,

death can feel like a dream

and I am nightgowned, perching on the bed's edge
in Sean's Midas room, string of fairy lights

hand-colored gold. I am manic and in love
with planning our escape. His absent smile,
impossibly hip. No real shock there.
My insistence on loving some light
into our tired eyes. My shaved head's debut
to rave reviews.

Icarus

Before Nathan lit me
on fire, before he walked
into the desert shimmer
& became a stone, before
I cupped flight like water
in my palms, I cast two spells—

      this is how you braid hair too short to grasp
      this is how you are a woman in a boy's coat.

Between Virgo & Libra is the Cusp
of Beauty, a city of unlanding birds.

I kiss the cacti
& remember what I've been
besides a ruby throat:

      barn owl in a fig tree// hawk
      lifting a snake from the grass//
      bat// thrush// gull// a pelican
      desperate for its dead kin,
      piercing its own heart.

Swollen Empty

When the meltdown came, it smelled
red. Smoke the color of thunder.
The sirens are teaching me. This is how to panic
before you've met truth. My sisters and I tangle
like weeds in this heat. We're getting bad
at the business of belief. Our stomachs swollen
and empty. I caught the last goose in the shallows.
Her feathers came off in my hand. Her youngest children,
capsized and bleeding. We didn't eat her.
I found her new eggs, like pearls. Perfect
white eyes rolled back.

Conditional

At twenty I miscarried a child.
He would be school-aged now,

a terror on your hip. Instead
he dissolved like a clot kissed with aspirin.

I blame the brandy and the wine. Not
foolish enough to call it *miracle*,

I would've kept the bastard in my bed
if he had grown beyond a seedling. I'd be wrong

to think my recklessness a rescue. My boy
full of loose teeth. I won't call it relief

when liquor stings the cut. He could've been aspirin,
a foolish kiss. He could've been

a rich meal slumped and stirring
in my stomach. Not three bloodless months

I paid no mind. Not a rosary of weeks
I thought my choices still immaculate.

He could've grown up a monster. Could've been bad
as the bastard who never knew I bled his baby.

I won't talk about my future like that. Conditionally. I won't worry
my wishing with a name I chose before I knew

what I'd be losing.

Butchery for the Blue Moon

It happened only once, in the doorway
between December and new circumstance.

I befriended the spoons. Drank from the pot of cider
simmering on the stove. Sat out the argument. Paced the porch

without a coat. The cold cut deep enough to keep
me on my feet. Someone narrated my past

between hiccups. Someone else fell from a cab
with a massive suitcase. Another still

vomited down a storm drain. And I got my apology, though
it came with pupils fine as fork tines.

It continued on the shuffle home through almost-snow.
He could not stop giving new names to his wrong,

shaking it by an ankle like a bird with throat cut.
Every feather blown down the avenue.

Meat of the old year, naked, bloodless,
flesh still warm in my hands.

I almost left him. Almost did
more than just finger the knife.

de Los Muertos

Feed the dead with smoke, with silk
sleeves and thin-soled shoes. Feed them
bone and feathered color. Play
donkey with the dead. Carry them
on your back like a cloak. Pedro the Sorcerer,
keeper of earthquakes. Eduardo's father, his music
and snakes. Feed them bundled sage, painted
bottles of agave. And the Spanish my own father spoke
only to my sister, words with slick clay seams between them.
The language you slow and keep, passing it between your hands,
nearly ripe fruit. The sleep of apples. A city of florists missing
the right blooms. Skull with a marigold mouth.

Good Time Girls

We sit down on the carpet.
Us two, the only girls
ever invited.

Smashing Pumpkins "1979"
looping as boys fill the room
with lean breath. Richard. Dave. Dru.
Rupert. Garrett. Riad. Army of the lost
holds a tactical meeting on how best to die
before the burnout. Skateboards? Acid?
Tepid QuikCheck coffee? The basement is as hot
& crowded as my tongue is in my mouth.

See them, lanky weeds
willing to go & grow up anywhere.
John Poverty, tattooing grapefruits,
then his own thigh, then the insides
of offered lips. Sean rank with chemical
roses from the perfume factory.
Joey, on a flight to Lithuania
in a few hours, banished
to a country without vowels.

And us two, compact, backs against the unmade bed.
She steals my notebook, writes in whisper script
I've had sex with too many people
in this room. I grab & hold her writing hand
wanting to absorb the panic of a place
with no mystery left.

When I'm Bad, I'm Better

The first time
somebody called me

a slut, I was not present.
I was somewhere wet

being a mermaid. I was
busy with black magic,

being burned alive
for the sound of my voice

in a sailor's conch
ear. I was the conch,

an island delicacy. You heard
I fuck with my eyes

open, you heard I fuck
anyone with hands, you heard

I fuck like a winner on the first day
his tides have turned, you heard

I fucked somebody (not you)
and shouldn't I be sorry

for the times I fill myself
with any violence at hand

even if that's just sticks and stones. I'll sink
I'll burn white heat I'm drowning

deep in the sea without gills. You aren't
welcome. My body isn't yours.

Vagrant Magic

Take back your knife. Blood is not the only road
to a heart. Spells can be cast; letters buried. Once, I broke
a window and he called it sex. Once, I drank the South

down like a gutter gulps the rain. He says *orphan*, but
there's an answer for that: in his shadow, you can see every country
where he's walked barefoot. When homeless, he prays

to any harbor that will have him. Makes saints of all
his empties. God doesn't like it when we leave the light on
but I can't sleep. He fell into it again—with a paper lantern,

a church steeple, a whiff of jasmine tea passing our table.
The haunting bleeds into the sheets. Once, I pressed
my lips to wet paint. A spell cast to steal the world

trailing in his wake. I am alone
when he says it—the quiet nothing that liquored
tongue found best at rest's doorstep. *You would*

be mine . . . bliss hinged on hesitation. No trees here. No low-
hanging fruit. No snake to blame my hunger on. Love comes
too late, a forked truth. He wrote me two letters. First, *I cannot stand*

the way your skin shifts like fuel under a flame.

Then, *You will never leave my mouth.*

Sailor's Knot

The first pull doesn't come like a kiss
undressing the mouth into muscle.
The first pull is a simple weight,

a body next to me in bed.
Weight, what sleeps and wakes me, salted
whisper sewn through every time of day.

Mornings, it is garlic hissing
in the kitchen, love bare to the waist
cradling an egg yolk in slack fingers.

Midday I am bare feet and stung shoulders.
Weight keeps me planted in the sand,
a slip of misplaced gold. The water attacks,

retreats, attacks. Weight tows me
into foam endlessly no matter how icy
or angry or needled the surf.

Nights, I am a siren dooming my own departure.
There's sand everywhere. My clothes are heavy with it
and the leaving. That pull, after the causeway,

comes like breath in my ear. The whisper
won't stay any longer than I let it. But
I do. I let it stay.

I'll Admit It

Right now my heart & your heart are taking bong rips,
giggle-cuddling, hoping one will kiss the other by accident.
They are stupid, smitten with smoke. Accidents do happen
after all. Bands break up on tour; best friends fuck
the same confused girl. Nothing sacred but the spells
that spin the world in reverse. Take time out of the equation.
Nothing dies, & nothing's dead. Imagine we are kings
holding court where the taxidermy chews on the houseplants
& all our past loves are still loyal. Our hearts, too stoned to chase
that daydream. Right now my heart wants to go dancing in new shoes.
On the drive home I see the buck that's haunted me across seven states.
Head bent to lick the salted road. Six points. I swerve, think
I've killed him. Ripped the antlers from his velvet head,
pickled his silent tongue. Another accident. But
he leaps off & all I can imagine is how ready I'd been
to pull him off the car's grille, to cut away his skin,
to sew it new with a crescent needle & two glass eyes.

Thick as Thieves

You fall asleep in the middle of
a party. Not an invitation to most
girls, but I buckle under the weight
of stillness. Hover. One stolen moment
given wings. Would've been easier to keep
the sun on my tongue than not touch. You, Puck
spilling flowers into eyes. Beneath that beard-softened jaw,
a clutch of teeth. You are still unbruised, what
the snake gave, the one I dream most often, doorway
in my sleep. A dare rises in our throats. I cast a girl off
a cliff, skin the neighbor's cat, leave my scarf at the bar,
handprints on your car's hood, fingers hooked into each buttonhole.

The dream shifts—weather strips the tree line, every limb
an avenue of blood. We run through corn on city feet,
syrup season gone. We die naked as the branches. You kiss me
under Dickinson's window—the Amherst spook blushes
waxed, sacred as sin. Sleep, the only place I can still
find you naked. That cruel tyrant feast—rich, rotting.
Before I can eat, some will spoil. You change
from a plug of tobacco to a skipping
rock to a handful of seed. The places you're harbored
spin through me like a zoetrope. You are not a man
but an idea, a flicker. The trees remind me of nothing
when they bloom. We walk away from the fire like criminals.

& when the canary stops singing

I curse that death. Carry it in a cage like a bird.
Marry it. Name the belt & dagger a man now

in the sky. Orion painted with soot. Marry him.
Sleep on his chest, that starry mouth in your hair.

Offer my lip & pray for blood. Offer a vein.
When I'm too afraid to watch, witch my sight.

Catch the ghost in glass. What can I see?
Is it how I loved the last one who bled

me like a lamb, hand on my head, saying
do not blame me for the blade? I drown the past

down the mine, hold it under until it jerks & screams.
Water howls if it rises quick. Me too. Me, blue

at the wrist. No yellow feather. I've offered
plenty, been shucked like an oyster. This is how

a girl gets wanted. Pull me through your teeth like smoke.
A cough. A coin in sand. A coal man's homely bride.

Wedding Soup

When I was a girl
and you were a girl
we were floral
and ungiveable. Squash

blossom. Bleeding
Hearts in the sideyard.
Vine, albino root. Petals
open only in the moonlight.

Then we were men.
It got easy—we ate curries
on Thayer, wore hats in summer,
wandered nights unchaperoned
as Providence became unbearably young
again. Our gutter spit, our busy hands.
Our teeth, aching out smiles.
Our unscandalous skin.

When I was a woman, I wasn't.
Wasn't flinch or furnace. Not mist
or down, not soft enough to settle on.
You were a nymph and I was an echo.
You, a letter and I, the lipstick.
I waited for you in the wrong skin.

The suitor—stuttering,
unsuitable.

Me, a boy
on skinned knee.
No bouquet or corsage.
Backwards and thorny
as a Bible Belt prayer.

In an instant, in the kitchen,
we are girls again—snow-damp,
wilted. I am cherry-stained
teeth. You are
the absence of *yes*.

Rosary for the Blood Moon

when the night rusts into its fifth season
of shredded skin

when the sky is a wine spigot
and my mouth, open

when the current slows in the wrong place
and the water is rigid as rope

when the ground is soft to the touch, giving
like skin under heat

when I beg for blooming cherry trees preserved
just as they were the month I vanished

when he says he saw a mare on Sunday
and she was good as my ghost

when the mirrors break
and we sweep the glass

when tangerines drop from their branches
into our open, empty hands

when we are our own children, and theirs too,
all generations blessed with sweet rind

when we have lost nothing except
what's been given away

in the name of my father, the sun,
and the spirit of what waiting

remains,
amen

Alpha

Sweat pearling like prayers in a novena. Some hurts are ugly
enough to dance with anyway. Some women are wolves.
I weave between her teeth like a howl. Like sinew.
This is how the wave will break: bold and brine
across her cheekbone. Kiss sewn through every pulse.
Her height in hours. Her hand in mine. The night, caught
in a single breath, a moth seduced by artificial light.

Twice, Praying

In the stairwell where
somebody was forever
strumming or passing a flask
down to the next landing, where
we were the youngest, most
volatile constellations—shifting so
rapidly we hijacked the tides
of an entire season, stilling
the breakwater a flat pane of glass—
I learned every word to that Nico song about
getting unstuck in time & that was what we were working at
so recklessly, that slippage from other people's children into our own
perfected monsters, the kind to beg back memories as if we loved
only in other, already-dead lives. But we loved more than just
how old we weren't, got young with stumble, forgot the words
on purpose as an excuse to try each verse on a second time,
leaning into when the lyric doubled back again,
avoiding the long return to where
we never planned to stay.

In My Blood Like Holy Wine

It's hideous, how true I've been
to my memorized ideal.

There are no levies for this, only rain to twist me
senseless. I'm barking at the glowing sky because maybe

we still live on the same planet. Maybe if I'm a dog, he'll hold me,
or if I'm a witch I can take the ocean in with a whip stitch and wander

through the shallows. I'm scrying for the right spell. Give it here
boy. Braid your fingers close to my neck and stay. Bee sting me

welted. I'll call it clover. I'm still stupid as the day
I fumbled my chopsticks into the Udon and it's true

that nothing I've eaten since the spring when we were starved
knives sharpening each other tastes quite rich enough

to blot him out. By September none of my cells will remember
this city the way he taught it: a rabbit crushed

into a bottomless satin hat.
Now, you see it. Now, it's hope.

Questing Beast

I'm scrubbing milk from my silver boots when I see it
                 winging from the corner of my eye—

    willful (they say)
bored with stillness,
          uncatchable as
             a breaking wave

     & before I can find a reason not to
I'm running full tilt on my bad right knee,
      knotting a gray-lunged decade into a snare

                   here's your net, my butterfly
              here's your daughter, Pelican

       come & bleed now, quiet
     while I fish in your throat for it

       the shoulder throne I rode
(Athena sprung from your skull & steering
     us both
             down River Road until it turned Columbus
    Avenue past muddy reservoir & became our bastard home)
the stone, rolled away   you coming back,

limping & sorry,
    to me

        I am imperfect & unwilling
     & running   still
        there's no space inconvenient
           for my shame

you're dead & I hate it   if I catch this vanishing creature long enough
        to ask my myth back into being

        the milk will spill a second time:
        a nest of graceless
        children begging father *feed me*
          feed me / starve yourself
           so I'll always be
          singing

Acknowledgments

Thanks to the editors of the following journals, in which many of these poems appeared (some in earlier forms or under different titles):

Amethyst Arsenic, Animal, apt, The Bakery, Banango Street, Blast Furnace, Carnival, Cactus Heart, FRiGG, Gigantic Sequins, ILK, Kudzu, Luna Luna, The Misanthropy, Muzzle, Nailed, Neon, OVS, [PANK], Paper Darts, The Pedestal, Prick of the Spindle, SHAMPOO, similar:peaks::, Split Rock Review, Sugar House Review, Sundog Lit, Super Awesome Mega Gigantic Pretty Sweet Friend Zine, tagvverk, Vector, Weave, The Well & Often Reader, Whiskey Island, wicked alice, Word Riot.

Thanks to Cassandra de Alba for suffering through seven years' bad luck with me, & for hearing & helping with more drafts than anyone. Endless gratitude for lighting the way, & the word "rind."

Thanks to Sean Patrick Mulroy for his unbelievably generous dedication of time & editorial energy to this project, for forcing me to write poems before I knew what to say, for nipping at my heels whenever the work felt too heavy & reminding me to witness anyway.

Thanks to KMA Sullivan, for mothering this beast into the world with me, & to Stevie Edwards, for looking me in the eye & calling me necessary.

Thanks to Hampshire Slam Collective, Boston Poetry Slam, Feral Bitch Palace, Pink Door & the Boston Center for Adult Education for growing me as a writer & editor, as well as an advocate for my own stories & the stories of others.

Thanks to my family, both blood & chosen, but especially the following for the sparks they cause in my brain & their relentless support: Kathy, Kaitlin, Chrissie, Owen, Lady, Strega Gianni, John Mortara, Emily Cataneo, Anna Meister, Sophia Holtz, Andy Locke, Aly Pierce, Kat Mott, Jericha Senyak, Emily Carroll, Zeke Russell, Sam Teitel, Mark Palos, Mckendy Fils-Aime, Melissa Newman-Evans, Justin Nixon, Erick Armbrust, Muggs Fogarty, Caroline Harvey, Jonathan Weiskopf, Rachel McKibbens, Erich Haygun, Lewis Mundt, Carlos Williams, & Grant Bonnier.

And thank you Sean Owen, for finding ways to feed me even now.

Notes

"The Ballad of Sexual Adventure" was written in response to photographer Nan Goldin's series entitled "The Ballad of Sexual Dependency." The italicized text in the poem has been repurposed from the lyrics to Charli XCX's "Take My Hand."

"Born to Die" borrows its title and much of its vocabulary from the Lana Del Rey album of the same name.

"Rusalka" takes its title from a type of freshwater mermaid found in Eastern European folklore, typically a woman who has been drowned or committed suicide by drowning just before her wedding day.

The quotations attributed to Winona and Susannah in "The Age of Instability" come from the narration in *Girl, Interrupted* (1999).

The phrase "the sleep of apples" in "de Los Muertos" comes from Cassandra de Alba's unpublished translation of Lorca's poem "Ghazal of the Dark Death"/"Gacela de la Muerta Oscura."

"When I'm Bad, I'm Better" takes its title from Mae West in *I'm No Angel* (1933), where the full moment of dialogue is, "When I'm good, I'm very good. But when I'm bad, I'm better."

"In My Blood Like Holy Wine" takes its title from the lyrics to Joni Mitchell's "A Case of You."

The creature referred to in the title of "Questing Beast" first appeared in Arthurian legend as a symbol of violence and chaos, though it appears elsewhere in literature as a symbol of Christ similar to the pelican.

EMILY O'NEILL was born on the bedroom floor in her mother's childhood home and has been making loud messes ever since. She is a writer, artist, and proud Jersey girl, but owes her poetry education to Cambridge's Cantab Lounge, home of the Boston Poetry Slam. She has facilitated workshops and poetry programming as a founding member of the performance troupe No More Ribcage and teaches creative writing at the Boston Center for Adult Education. Her first collection, *Pelican*, won the Pamet River Prize from YesYes Books and her work has been featured in *The Best Indie Lit New England*, *Sugar House Review*, and *Whiskey Island*. Her poem "de Los Muertos" was selected by Jericho Brown as the winner of *Gigantic Sequins*'s second annual poetry contest. She has a degree in the synesthesia of storytelling from Hampshire College and lives in Medford, MA with a coven of feral women writers and their gigantic orange tabby, Roger Mindfucker.

Also from YesYes Books

VINYL 45S

A PRINT CHAPBOOK SERIES

Pepper Girl by Jonterri Gadson

Bad Star by Rebecca Hazelton

Still, the Shore by Keith Leonard

Please Don't Leave Me Scarlett Johansson by Thomas Patrick Levy

No by Ocean Vuong

POETRY SHOTS

A DIGITAL CHAPBOOK SERIES

Nocturne Trio by Metta Sáma

[ART BY MIHRET DAWIT]

Toward What Is Awful by Dana Guthrie Martin

[ART BY GHANGBIN KIM]

How to Survive a Hotel Fire by Angela Veronica Wong

[ART BY MEGAN LAUREL]

The Blue Teratorn by Dorothea Lasky

[ART BY KAORI MITSUSHIMA]

My Hologram Chamber Is Surrounded by Miles of Snow by Ben Mirov

[IMAGES BY ERIC AMLING]